STRANGE MUSIC OF BONE

STRANGE MUSIC OF BONE

Andrew Hawthorne

KATABASIS

First published in 1998 by KATABASIS
10 St Martins Close, London NW1 0HR (0171 485 3830)
Copyright © Andrew Hawthorne 1998
Printed and bound by Antony Rowe Ltd,
Chippenham (01249 659705).

Typeset in-house mainly in 12 point Garamond Antiqua
ISBN: 0 904872 30 0

Trade Distribution: Central Books
99 Wallis Road
London E9 5LN
0181 986 4854

British Library Cataloguing in Publication Data:
A catalogue record for this book is available
from the British Library.

KATABASIS is grateful for the support
of the London Arts Board.

For
Emilia Grace

ACKNOWLEDGMENTS

Some of these poems have appeared in the following journals and magazines: *English, South, Iota, Target, The Radical, The Grendon Grail, Christian Poetry Review, Handshake, Dandelion, Christchurch Parish News, Blithe Spirit, Quirk, Poetry Now, Poetry Today, The Dorchester Guardian, Smiths Knoll, Smoke, Tears in the Fence, Brass Butterfly;* and in the following anthologies: *Contemporary English Poetry I, Songs of the Cross, The Killing, The New Forest Poetry Society Anthology, Reclaiming the Nails, Spiritual Journeys* and *The Star-laden Sky.*

The author and publisher are grateful to the Dorset Natural History and Archaeological Society at the Dorset County Museum for permission to use the photographs of the Durotrigian Burial for the front cover and of the portrait of William Barnes for the back cover.

CONTENTS

I
Bones

II
The Losing of Childhood

III
A Private Autumn

IV
Against the Beast

I
Bones

William Barnes walks his Parish

At times he disturbed the grass on their tumuli
as he collected his parishioners' tithes and vowels.

He knew that under his feet
was a strange music of bone
which was echoed under every thatch in his parish.
And their blood which cried to him
more insistently than Abel's
was warmed still at each hearth as he looked by,
although theirs left no more than a stain
in the soft chalk,
if at all.

From Maumbury Ring to Herringston Barrow
the mute ancestors lay tracing destinies
in the palm of their bony hands as he walked by.
They listened to their children
as he recited their stories into a poem,
suggested improvements,
acquiesced,
offered him a strange harvest of songs.

The Ancestor known as Excavation 10221
13.1.88 Skeleton SF 3030
1x1 N O.B. 50mm
DCM Accession 1996.30.13.WW221.3030
Photograph W221 33/19

A skeleton is unearthed from its grave during the construction of the Dorchester by-pass

For Olivia Bell, and Peter and Ann Woodward

1

You unmask him with
your sable-tipped watercolour brush.
You flick the earth grains into your cupped palm
and reveal the holes that were his eyes.
He stares silently, sees you examine
your hands in the light,
is grateful for your shadow against the sun.

2

Brown earth seasoned in good loaming, his
soil-filled rib-cage subsides into the chalk
like a ship's keel in a gentle sea road
or his own hand testing the quern flour,
leaving fingerprints.
He sees the same rooks fly overhead,
understands their squawking.
The ridgeway to the south is tenantless but familiar,
houses gone under the earth,
unharvested crops grow wild now.

3

A hole in his skull you could put your fist in.
Some do, expecting epiphany,
finding instead soil. Club or sword split
spade crush or earthmover, ard or plough shaved,
ancient wound once blood graced
or the colourless seep of generations, worms
and roots.

4

1.5 mtrs, teeth intact if worn
implying good nourishment. Between 35 and 40
Excavation 10221 is a typical round-hole
Durotrigian burial

whose bony hand, if you overlay it with your own,
is quickly warmed.

---

ard = primitive plough

The Archeologist at Maiden Castle

He felt the wind pause on his face.
North wind,
keeper of ice, eyes smarting
he turned again.

He passed
the earth raised circles of their homesteads
the cold hearths, the door post holes
revealed in dark earth
to his trowel
and the horse's jaw bone planted at midnight
for an incredible tree
beyond the reach of his digging,
and the generations of supplications
muttered into cupped hands
were silent.

He heard
the hearth whispers
and the susurrus of the quern

the telling of old stories
polished like old bronze at its touching
or the invention of fresh
and unfamiliar landscapes,
stumbling tongues on new vowels
foreign, harsh
breaking of ploughs on new rock
a shattering of customs

and the wolf cry in the sudden night
the smoke blown night
suddenly silent

and he passed on.

Thomas Hardy Inspects the Building Site of his New House, Max Gate

Here is the ancient floor,
Footworn and hollowed and thin,
Here was the former door
Where the dead feet walked in.

THOMAS HARDY, The Self-Unseeing

He had known the burials were there, and
the presence of bone pleased him. The hollow tibia
would be flutes to his music, past and present charmed
in the jigs and reels his ancestors danced
on the ridgeway barrows he would see from his
bedroom window.

(At every sun-cast their vibrant figures
disappeared over the hill,
long shadows on ancient earth,
and these were comforting to this time-torn man.)

But when the drain diggers struck rock
which had a certain smoothness
and channels cut which eased the dripping water
from its surface,
the dry bones fell silent. Staring into the hole
he saw the firelight red on upturned faces
and the suppliant hands eager with corn offerings
for the sunrise through spectral mists.
He saw the knife
poised and the blood-red lips
rich with the syllables of prayer.

He felt the hid-heart loosening crimson
over the sarsen stone, cooling towards the edge,
sheening ruby over her votive gold,
sealing the earth at his feet.
He nodded and agreed the extra men to lift it,
left instructions for its care, confused the labourers
with his concern for useless rubble.

On leaving, he measured his footfalls
to his future hearth,
undertook to move it slightly to the east,
hoped it would be enough.
He was content to share his house with ghosts,
would enjoy their silences, seek
his reflection in their proud brief eyes,
take evening walks over their graves.

Hardy discovered that Max Gate was being built over a site of intense ancient activity. The grounds of his new house included a Durotrigian cemetery, as well as a causewayed enclosure, a Round Barrow and a stone placement, which Hardy described as 'the Druid Stone'. This stone now stands within the garden of Max Gate, and a replica may be seen in the Dorset County Museum.

Sun-cast, time-torn, hid-heart, and spectral mists are all phrases from Hardy's poems.

I am indebted to Peter Woodward for telling me the history behind Max Gate.

In Memoriam R. S. Thomas

With language learnt from an unearthed skull
with a stone tongue
still soil stained, its shine taken by the clay
robbed and redacted from the tombs of
Llandogo, Llanigon, Llansilin, Llan-y-pwll,
ap-Williams, ap-Jones, ap-Tudor, ap-Thomas
anybody, nobody,
Neb

the poet speaks furiously
in his mother's voice, breast-fed vowels
under an English cloak
in a London suburb

his own history
of being a lion in a dragon's skin

under the larkwing in the voiceless air.

Markings

I heard your whispers count
the undoing days around the roots
of bowing grasses.

You had often walked this way, to carry
your pail of frozen water home
to melt the work's grime.

Earth and root slime and the dust
of old bones compounded anonymously
and swept with the strife of the plough
over huge distances.

Only the tramp of a dozen generations
kept it clear, and when the pail spilt
it revealed brown mirrors in the stones
and was quick to seep through.

Fear of Drowning in the New Forest

We sit in our car at the end
of the new sand enclosure.

Other families come. Their children, running,
are told to keep the car in sight.

Larksong moors itself by ribbons to the earth.
No larks are seen.
The horses wander, riderless.

Here the undernavigated soil
is scarred by streams to its white ribs.
Here the grazing
is tide flecked with the bones and twigs
of a murmuring history
over-peopled in its solitude.

We see in the gorse-bounded horizons
limitless ocean. Clouds float and subside.
Children's cries like those of drowning men.

Blackberrying

We gather September's dead.
Stubble smoke winds us in thin shrouds.
Berry stains mingle with pricked blood
which we exchange reaching for the same fruit.

Bees quicken, change
summer to their colony's survival,
die beneath flowers they craved.

Hazel and sloe and rowan and elder
leave their young as offering and retreat
fearing the first frost

while the heat haze under a virgin sky
excites the plough furrows into consciousness
and from their stavelines
the ancient music rises silently.

We take our tears that were confusion of smoke
and pricked fingers.
We take a basket of fruit
that seethes with escaping insects.
Our blood we leave drying on the thorns.

Pub Lunch, Cerne Abbas, Dorset

Under the tumuli patient bones
brood while sifted by the seep of rain
and roots and time.
Rabbit, mole, badger, fox keep secret vigil.
Perhaps we disturb them with our whispering.
Their departure is silent.

Two roads into the village
bequeathed us the familiar option
and this time we chose the sunken lane
raftered in deep shadows
cut into the October afternoon
and the mist which was a confusion
of autumn and woodsmoke.

Woodsmoke from the hearth fire:
logs splitting, yielding their time:
if we are quick enough we can count their years
in disappearing rings, soon embers and ash.
They offer themselves, wheezing time in frail incense
and raising our remembrance of other days like this.
We will take their fragrance
home in our clothes and hair.

Kissing Bones: On the body of Uzzi, the Bronze Age Man

Discovered on a mountain pass, Switzerland, 1991,
and now in various universities around the world.

1

Curse of this ice: my immaculate preservation.
To thaw is to pry: my last meal,
colour of eyes, a unique finger print
the cut of my axe: the Bronze Age personality.

How I yearn for the earth, its
anonymity, disappearance of flesh
stain of bone in the soil's palm
or a grubby flint shard overlooked at their raking,
sift of root crawl and worm, a proper death.

2

Parcelled between nations my flesh
like wind-blown seed germinates
beneath their carbon dating eyes.
My blind progeny. To seek only age
and diet: an irrelevant harvest.

Dig of scalpel's cold steel.
in their sterile fingers
the yield of my crop
(the warmth of kinship in the bone's cup,
premonition of their own humanity)
prised like tares from a field of corn.
A second death.

The Story of Olaf Bjornson

When they landed the botanists
thought the Norwegian spruce
a little erratic,
in Madagascar.

The local people looked at the strangers
in disappointment
from their steel-blue eyes,
which also intrigued them.

How could they know
(not knowing the language)
that the trees had grown
from the grave of Olaf Bjornson
who came to the island in a green-timbered long-boat
and a pocketful of pine-cones
the only food left for his voyage
a thousand years ago.

He became revered as a god
full-rigged and well-endowed
giver of iron and wearer of a lion's mane on his chin
said to work miracles of fertility on young girls
who were given strands of the gold
growing on his head
and a pine-cone as a necklace for a blessing.

His boat was inverted and used as the royal palace
until he died. They gathered around him each night
and listened intently to his stories from the North,
telling by the craggy vowels
and the tears which shimmered in the fire-light

the terrors of the sea and the horror of exile.
After the glowing of the embers some stayed,
usually women.

They buried him under an approximation
to Norwegian funeral songs
and his long-boat.
The women covered his body
with strands of his own hair
and laid the pine-cones as a crown around his head,
just deep enough in the soil
for Olaf to sprout into a dozen trees,

tall, strong gods

which became various research papers
and long conversations over dinner at high table,
proof of the erratic forces of nature,
strong currents and good fortune.

To the King of the Sutton Hoo Ship Burial

Where timbers are dark shadows
and bone survives cast in crumbling sand
I seek you.

Plough strifed and robbed
and sifted by a thousand years of
rain and rootcrawl, worm reach
and ignorance, you leave

a shattered but proud sword.
A crushed helmet.
A coagulation of rusted chain mail.
And a few drops of exquisite gold,
offerings you left for us to use

and a whetstone against which we sharpen
our reputations,
or a few poems

and some crouched dragons and eagles
perpetually ready for flight. Ossified
motifs for the broken lyre now done.
Laughter as you took the wind.

You are sailing now, ghost
and ghost boat, safe
from the gravediggers.
But you leave your shadows
playing in the sand for us.

Abbot Skulin Looks out of his Cell Window during a Storm

The wave warped skies, the burning skua
that lies over the petrel, porpoise
and seal road safe now from the harrowing keel,
unknown cries and salt you find in your clothes
and hair the next morning,

these are paced, and paced
around his cell in prayer. His old cloak yielding years
in each fold, practising for his grave shrouding,
the abbreviated Psalter whose rough gall ink
explodes at the spatter of each rain drop
across its vellum,
these are his grave goods in a fine season,
the wind and the fat rain

making the earthen floor rich mud under his window.
At every pacing
another footprint, overlaying another, until
a whole army passes. These are his legacy

his brothers find in the morning, becoming
in time a legion of angels, or perhaps
a Viking raid ship feverish for spoil
in the eye of a storm,

leaving, strangely, no corpses.

The Last on the Tyne

The old ships weep themselves away
in rusty water.
They return from where they came.

The shipbuilders cannot return.
They are where they are.
The No Job Centre taunts them
with prospects in the South
securing Twyford
and Newbury
and Salisbury for by-passes. Go south.
Become people who are not
where they are.

II
The Losing of Childhood

My Son, my son

My son is always agitated
until he is let out into the garden
through the french windows in the morning.

He sits in the garden seat
and stares in at us, at peace.
His footsteps in the dew are erased by the sun.
Blackbirds play at his feet.

His hands open in his lap are offered
neither in prayer nor greeting
entreating merely of distance.

Noon and sunset. Dusk
gathers our day's achievements,
visits, letters, funerals, poems. We
stand at the window. My eyes
meet his across the garden; more shadow
than recognition. We raise our hands
and mouth a calling.
The light's put on.
I stare back at myself in the blinded glass.

The Losing of Childhood

You remember
the ascent from the beach
on the hair-pin path
which revealed your abandoned sand-castle
at every bend when we looked back.

It disappeared by instalments
as in a series of time-lapse photographs
capturing the tide's chase
of its shadow up the sand.
As we paused and rested at each turn
its ramparts turrets keep and moat
had oozed a little more back to the sea.

We thought it amusing, then tried to hoist a smile
when we saw your tears.
There will be other beaches, more castles,
we promised you. Grander, stronger,
more memorable.

But not this one again, you said,
not this one.

On the Beach

The ice-cream girl smiles at me
beneath her mirror shades.
I notice purple nail varnish as she passes over
my 99. Our fingers touch, hers
slip imperceptibly from beneath mine,
are surprisingly warm.

I offer £5, eager for change.
She drops the coins into my hand,
stares beyond me to the next.

We all go down to the dark.
I am not reflected in her eyes.

Cliff Top

From your cliff top house you saw
a school of dolphins
dress the sun with rainbows at their leaping.
Cormorants and porpoises were observed also,
although these were less metaphysical.

Then one evening alerted by its chugging diesel
spinning hanks of sound to your bedroom window
you saw the hired fishing boat *The Endeavour*
four points east and looking back,
filled with the silhouettes of former friends,
waving perhaps.

Lost on my Neighbour's Ocean

My neighbour probably knows
the tide never reaches his back garden
but he sits in his boat just the same.

Although you can hear the herring gulls
and pretend the wind in the trees is an ocean
it takes more than a little imagination
to see the wave spume and feel
the salt spit in a border of dahlias.

At night he lights a candle
and puts it in a jam-jar on a broomstick
he calls a mast.

To warn the other shipping, he answers.
Or if I'm lost adrift with the engine down
to summon help —
you can never tell.
I promise to keep him informed
of the shipping forecast,
provide him supplies when he's next in port,
feed his cat until his return.

Digging

My neighbour is always digging in his garden.
I see him every time I look
through the holes in our fence. He wears flares
and a yellow dufflecoat even in July,
anticipates fashion every twenty years.

My wife once stood on a chair on Christmas day,
looked over the fence, asked him in for a sherry.
No thank you, he said, I have to finish here.
It helps pass the time. Since mother died, time drags.
The potatoes will be up before the year is out,
leeks too, and the chicken bones I planted
will sprout next Easter into an incredible tree.
Your husband will notice it
when he looks through the fence,
you'll see.

Flying Kites in Cloud

In memory of Ron Huckle, kite-flyer,
whom I buried 26th March 1998

The kite man replied,
I'm angling an upturned ocean
where crows skim the cloud rim
like flying fish over the wave's prow,
and where the whale-song is usurped
by Tristars slipstream-wrapped in distance.

It takes great skill, he said, to pilot a kite
through such tides and currents with only
your hand to judge the depth. And when I reel it in
what weed, what fish, what crabs and lobsters
shall we trawl?
What once deck-raftered bone?

The 10:02

There is a man with a cello.
He is arguing that it doesn't need a ticket.
But it takes a seat. But it's not a passenger.
I clear my throat. It's 10:01.

Along the platform I have time to see
tomorrow's newspapers dissolving in a puddle
and a crocodile between the rails singing an elegy
over the greenhouse effect.
It's nothing but a bad dream, he sings,
I can live here now.

The carriage jolts off.
Sixty seats. Fifty-eight pairs of eyes
avoiding each other reading books.
Another pair lock on to mine:
a man sat next to his cello. Come, he says,
sit next to me.
As long as I keep his cello on my lap.

Double

I met the man my mum says is my double.
Apart from specs he looks nothing like me.
He works in the Midland Bank.
He has a combination lock briefcase in black leather
and doesn't look as if he collects
backnumbers of *Playboy*.
When I introduced myself
he was polite if a little puzzled
and graciously accepted my invitation home to tea.

Oracle

I went to see the Bus Stop Man.
He waits all day in the shelter waving them on.
He never boards. There is no point, he answers;
he knows where they go; the shelters there
are identical.

A View from the Window

The buses pass in the night.
They are greenhouses growing people.
I stand at my window.
Sometimes I raise a hand.
Sometimes there is enough time
for them to see that I am here.

The Bee Factory

The bees multiply in our attic.
You call it the bee factory
and lie awake before the sun rises
remembering the summer they are busy
storing in their hive
enraptured like a gemologist reordering her collection.

I called the council pest control
and he came with his smoking pellets
and asked us to leave and the dog too.
On our return we found merely a faint smell of ether
and a large bill.
You have not quite forgiven me.

A Walk in the Country

After we have passed
the flies resettle on the path.
They sit and burn gently in the sun,
little emeralds with wings.
They wait to be disturbed again.

Saying Goodbye

The wasps are dying; they drone lazily like sighs,
impatient for their grave.

Over the fields we follow the crumbling furrows
which lie like stavelines in the ravished earth.
We raise the ancient music at our footfalls.
We've rehearsed this piece
always waiting for tomorrow
but that was yesterday;
we are lost in the reality between,
our tongues turned into the grey slate
which roofs the low squat cottages
abandoned to the silent owls.

We will part now, but we will stay.
Our shadows will clutter the empty soil,
seek each other at the lengthenings of dawn and dusk,
meet and elide. And turning different ways
into the sunken lane
we promise to write, to keep in touch, and forget.

A Man, having made a Journey

He thought the house unusually cool,
considering the kind of day they'd had.

Crows, carefully measuring their shadows
against the baked earth,
had kept their distance. Larks, too,
sacrificing to him it seemed
their ribbons of song
turning this way and that in the still air.

From his case he draws
a blunted knife, an untied knot of string,
a bag of cherry stones still wet.

He sits by the window, is eased
by the familiar creak of the chair,
looks back.
On the far hill-side their dying fires
are constellations brought to earth, the light
centuries old and decayed, bloated and cold.

Setting the lamp he sees
by the reflection in the dusty glass
a man much older,
and a caster of shadows.

The Policeman Remembers
the Crash Scene

What he remembered most vividly
was not the dried blood on the windscreen
flaking like old paint from a door.
Nor the burnt fingers which still gripped
the cigarette stub,
nor the *Playboy* centrefold spread open
on the passenger seat,
but
the way J. S. Bach on continuous play
sounded the same to the living and the dying.

III
A Private Autumn

Borderlands

I asked the ferry-man what the weather
would be tomorrow.

'A force nine but clearing
round Wicklow by noon; pillow-footed breezes
onshore, perhaps,
as far as the salmon road reaches
but becoming cyclonic by sundown;
precipitation, certainly, by the end of the year.

And when you gain the borderlands
turn back and remember me. The winters
will be longer for you; ice dreams itself
across the river over night
and in the same river the harvest moon
is shattered by the dragonfly seeking its birthplace
after a day's life. There, the morning light
wakes you in gentle stabbings,
and the long-dried wasps
drone over your head in attics overcrowded
with the affects of previous centuries

and those you used to know
who died last year
will shun you with sincere apologies.'

Mrs Oliver's Apple

Mrs Oliver lies staining her beetroot
and some of her blood has flecked the lettuces, too.
Mr Oliver lies buried like an old dried tuber
stored against the winter famine
in the Anderson shelter.
A direct hit, the neighbours say.

Shrapnel has pierced the greenhouse
giving the adequate ventilation
they had always desired.
The tomatoes will thrive now.

The children will come later
and collect the steel bomb-shards
and these will become heirlooms,
picked from the spot where No.19 used to stand,
be fondled occasionally, bleed rust into future palms.

On the pond the goldfish float.
The water spumed like a shattering chandelier,
subsided, became still.
It will be filled in and forgotten,
its outline in the soil fleshing the legend
of the Crater, the Exact Spot,
becoming also an unexplained muster point for cats.

The prize apple tree has disappeared.
There was never a crop as this year's, they said.
Mrs Oliver, giving way to her last temptation
before joining her husband underground,
was just reaching for one
when the five-hundred-pounder

landed like a wind-fall at its roots.
Apples were scattered with shrapnel
all over the neighbourhood
just in time for the late planting.
Some sprang up the next April,
eventually gave fruit which tasted
faintly metallic.

Fifty years on and Still Waiting

After he buried his wife
he returned every day to see if she'd sprouted.

They dug the hole too deep, he said.
The cold earth stole the vigour of her shoots
and she can't break the soil,
this year at least.

A Winter Tree

When dad brought the apple tree home
he pretended he didn't know which way up it went.
Do I plant this end or that in the soil?

My brother and I (being six and four)
couldn't tell him.
Branches could be roots and roots branches
with only a stick in between
the thickness of my little finger.

Dad winked, pretended to guess.
The feathery sapling was bedded
and we helped to tamp it in.
When you've grown up, we'll know, he said.
Perhaps roots will sift air
and in the fruit bowl
newly dug apples will have the scent of fresh earth.

A Visit in Convalescence

My father ripens on the bench,
an early windfall
wiped clean and put out in the sun.

My visit. We sit together in the heat.
I exchange a monologue for a nod.
The end's in sight.
He waits and wonders who'll be next.

Long Shadow of War

The sky outside your bedroom window
is eggshell blue cross-spun with broken spiders' webs.
In silence the airmen die,
spewing in blood their wives' or girlfriends' names,
confounding ground control with prayers and curses.
Their corpses float beneath
what seem to you white mushrooms, made of silk.
On the roof
the patter of shrapnel confusing you with rain.

A Private Autumn

Blind, your sleeping hand finds mine.
A gentle squeeze
like two leaves touching in the sun.

Tomorrow you won't remember this
and I won't tell you.
It's my little secret dream
in the palm of my hand,
just between the two of us.

Counting Clouds

He bequeathed you the counting of clouds
on a green afternoon, a hint of rain,
smoke from a leaf fire that shrouded you
in its winding sheet.

You did not want these. In a jaded sun
you choose to remember the smell of rain
in your hair
and the tears conjured by the burning,
a voice describing the sky.

He sometimes writes to ask
in letters increasingly atrophied
whether you learnt to tell cirrus from nimbus,
and if a leaf can cradle in its curling death
the summer which never was.

Lamplight

Those hands you clasped so tight together
on that first embarrassed photograph,

cool and gnarled in mine. As though
the sepia tint which blurred your early smile
darkens in the dust and rubbings of the years,
hides the shine, you say. You make me promise

to leave it hanging in your room,
beneath the lamp which lights it so awkwardly.

Elegy

You leave me your last breath,
quite empty hands on the cotton sheet,
a walnut face loosening in the afternoon sun.

You made me promise an elegant headstone,
real flowers, an echo in the retrochoir
enough to remind old priests of summer vespers
sung in Latin
and sunlight sifting clouds of incense
like an Annunciation.

You asked me to return to your photograph albums
and trace your gentle smile across the century
to the little child with a lapful of spring blossom
asleep in the shade of the apple tree.

March Burial

The bee forages amongst our blooms,
weaving an indiscreet path in primeval dance
from one grave to another while we in clusters
screen our tears, or lack of them.

It vibrates against our condolence cards,
rejects as useless our cellophane-wrapped
and borrowed epitaphs
guaranteed against the weather.

On the bee's wings instead sapphire and turquoise
transfixed
in the afternoon sun

as it takes pollen for its summer hive,
turning to nourishment
the yellow dust irritating on our overcoats.

IV
Against the Beast

A History of Helicopters from Vietnam to the Gulf War

In the susurrus of their rotorblades
the helicopters sing their disappearance
over their spawning.

Like departing locusts
leaving stripped fields
they guarantee corpses for twenty years.

Their eggs are laid.
Their larvae grow fat in spent shell cases
and the skulls of men
too young to die.

Holocaust

Bosnia disintegrates in a corner
of our living room. Smoke
and blood and bone nightly poured
in sacrifice: we number
the unintelligible dead. Then
the weather, then
the welcome bed.

5th November 1996

Mostar in my neighbour's garden.
His family are silhouetted
against the flames.
Crackle of small-arms fire across the city.
Explosions overhead
which are just shrapnel short of war.
Flares, maroons, tracer fire
banshee wails of the newly damned.

In my room standing at my window
I raise a hand.
They wave back, practising surrender.
Their children's cries like those of the dying.

The Music of the Spheres

1

Galileo felt the silent rhythm of the stars
and saw the hour that Newton's apple fell.

Halley saw his comet cast a shadow
over Bosnia. People looked at it and saw
not the signature of God in its fiery tail
but a sense of distance.
If this proved
the existence of God then he
was as elliptical as the comet's orbit
and just as useless.

2

Heisenberg knew the atoms in his brain
were perpetually uncertain
and proved it with a ream
of immaculate equations. He had no choice.

All the while he saw the Holocaust
and knew it was written in his mind's eye.

It all depends where you are watching from, he said.
Many of these particles are in the midst
of Being
and Not Being.

3

We inhabit the spaces left between,
a handful of quicksilver in God's palm,
a falling leaf from the apple tree

with nowhere to land.

Christchurch Priory

1

The Painter

Pig's blood and gold:
common elements of prayer.

A solemn, myopic invocation
at the first stroke; muttered curse
and contrition. A new devotion
at your fingertips.

Between the beech wood and paint
salvation and pain seared, martyrs'
vocation at the workbench
in a shaft of sunlight.

Then varnish and blessing.
A dream of saints
in glorious apotheosis.

2

Scriptorium

The grind of the bone and the black pig's blood
mixed with the sulphuric curses
of a dozen previous attempts

ooze over the bleached vellum. Word
after precise liturgical word
filling the page like the precentor's voice
overfilling the quire.

Soon the moment for the lead guide-lines
to be eased away
and the delicate application of the beaten gold
to be followed by a wash of lapis lazuli
and emerald: the all-important initial letter
the carcass of the text

complete. Then the drying,
the cut of the straight edge
the prayer of dedication at the altar,
the murmur of thanksgiving at the turn of the page.

3

The Urgent Contract

Brothers on the scaffold,
mason and glazier, tracery
and glass, finger and file
weaving an intimate tapestry.

Dawn to dawn, catching each mood
of the sun or the moon in rising glass
panel by panel translating light to liturgy.

Bloodshot eyes, monosyllables
echoing into the vaulting
moonshadow at play on the pillars

ease of the last lead
jointing glass to stone, two
quick prayers of dedication,
feel the flood of the nave at first light.

Jesus Falls for the Last Time

He sees his shadow
like a doorway into the night
darkening the road.

He smells the drain full of donkey piss
and cabbage leaves
and hears the scurrying of small, immediate creatures
under their canopy.

The jeers of the passers-by are strangely distant.
Looking up from this other realm
he sees their faces dissolving into the sun;
they are black shapes seeking each other in the dark.

Lifting himself off the ground
he discovers how like an old and weathered skull
a cobble stone feels in his palm.

The Soldier with the Spear

1

He noticed how quickly
blood dried on sun hot steel
on a silent afternoon.
The water had evaporated from the spear
like the tears from the eyes of the man's mother.
But the blood had stayed

and on its patina spreading over the blade he could see
a delicate rainbow of colours which twitched
and danced as he turned it in the light.

2

Blood on the sand
had dried to a blackness
he had not seen since the dead men's eyes
that stared at him still from foreign battlefields
in occasional dreams.

The water that had also dripped
had found a way between the grains; blood cloyed
too easily, blood stayed, blood stained,
would not leave
would not stay silent.
Perhaps, he thought, this water
would find desiccated tubers or a flower seed
dried beyond bone and bring life,
if only a little, but only to rise

to be trampled tomorrow.

Reclaiming the Nails

1

A good day's work.
Jewels of blood
coruscations of emerald blow-flies,
common coinage of Golgotha.
Early evening shift.
Reclamation of nails. Iron
too pricey to leave and rust.

2

Fingers stiffened
like a plaster god
dried in the mid-day sun. Tactile deity
dead in empty embrace.

3

Calloused hands like mine.
A working man. A carpenter,
they say; familiar then with the feel
of wood and cold iron;
death by occupation.

4

Coldness of touch.
Ease of the nail.
Blackened blood in withdrawal.
Blunted by the bone;
regrind in the morning. Another death
another sharpening of the nail.
One more day.

For Ken Saro-Wiwa

I stopped buying from Shell.
I bought from BP instead
and raped South America as well.

I poured petrol over your corpse
and applied the match.
I turned away when the smoke rose.
I tortured the earth they put you in.

I did not know. I did not want to know.
You lived in a country
in a geography text book
which is prone to such things.
You simply confirmed my opinions.

But the hands
that reach out to me from your grave
at my feet
are just like mine.
One still holds your pen
and the other is covered in blood.

I take your hand and pray
that your pen won't sleep in mine.

But will they listen to my poems, Ken?
Maybe the only writing they read
is my name when it doesn't appear
on the cheque or the switch-card slip.

But I listened. I heard your silent poem as they
dragged you to the scaffold.

I heard the smooth tongues
of the spades as they dug your grave
and the stamp of their boots
as they levelled the earth.

And we shall harvest your bones a thousandfold
from your soil.

By-Pass

'In the second week of the protest, the protesters are now trying a new trick. Evicted from their tents and taken down from the trees, they are now digging burrows underground.'

The Newbury Weekly News

On the eighth day
we took to the earth.

They had pillaged our houses
and pissed on our fires
and plucked us from the trees
like over-ripe fruits
containing all the knowledge they did not want.
Paradise was postponed
and on the cries we sent to the tree tops
they sharpened their chainsaws.

At night their silhouettes danced
around the fires
and their axes glinted smiles
at the thousand tree stumps left in the soil.
Their laughter rose in the smoke
and the cold ash settled on our faces.
In the morning we rose white-haired and wise
and took to the earth.

We dug into centuries of leaf-mould
and our spades gave voice to the mute bones.
We dug beyond the burrows of mice and voles
and the tangle of roots like a cat's cradle
and found
the broad dark river of loam.

We roomed there,
imagining vast labyrinths
we could lose them in,
easy to spot in their fluorescent coats
by the torchlight,
where black earth would silence their radios,
where the dampness
would seep into their bones.

They'll come.
We hear the earthmovers
baying at their heels.
We hear the concrete mixers belching their war cry
and their curses at having to dig us out.

They will Lazarus us from our voluntary tomb.
They will stand slightly in awe
as we crawl blinking into the sunlight,
casting regretful looks back to our womb of earth.
Some might applaud as we rise, but silently,
others will look us in the eyes
and remember us for the future.
Then we will part, each uncertain of the winner.